WHAT'S INSIDE ME?

My LUNGS

by Jennifer Wendt

BEARPORT
PUBLISHING

Minneapolis, Minnesota

Credits: Cover, all background, © Piotr Urakau/Shutterstock; cover, 7, 9, 23 © BlueRingMedia/Shutterstock; cover, 4, 9, 12, 16, 20, 22 lungs illustration © Shutterstock; all pages (doodles) Tiwat K/Shutterstock; 4 Africa Studio/Shutterstock; 5 Monkey Business Images/Shutterstock; 6 Matis75/Shutterstock; 7 Double Brain/Shutterstock; 8 SciePro/Shutterstock; 10 Art of Kosi/Shutterstock; 10 (tree) K.Sorokin/Shutterstock; 11 crystal light/Shutterstock; 12 Low Sugar/Shutterstock; 13 BlueRingMedia/Shutterstock; 14 Spectral-Design/Shutterstock; 15 airdone/Shutterstock; 17 Africa Studio/Shutterstock; 18 wavebreakmedia/Shutterstock; 19 Creativa Images/Shutterstock; 20 David Tadevosian/ Shutterstock; 21 Olena Yakobchuk/Shutterstock

President: Jen Jenson
Director of Product Development: Spencer Brinker
Senior Editor: Allison Juda
Associate Editor: Charly Haley
Designer: Oscar Norman

Library of Congress Cataloging-in-Publication Data

Names: Wendt, Jennifer, author.
Title: My lungs / by Jennifer Wendt.
Description: Fusion books. | Minneapolis, Minnesota : Bearport Publishing Company, [2022] | Series: What's inside me? | Includes index.
Identifiers: LCCN 2021048404 (print) | LCCN 2021048405 (ebook) | ISBN 9781636914435 (library binding) | ISBN 9781636914503 (paperback) | ISBN 9781636914572 (ebook)
Subjects: LCSH: Lungs--Juvenile literature.
Classification: LCC QM261 .W46 2022 (print) | LCC QM261 (ebook) | DDC 612.2/4--dc23/eng/20211001
LC record available at https://lccn.loc.gov/2021048404
LC ebook record available at https://lccn.loc.gov/2021048405

Copyright © 2022 Bearport Publishing Company. All rights reserved. No part of this publication may be reproduced in whole or in part, stored in any retrieval system, or transmitted in any form or by any means, electronic, mechanical, photocopying, recording, or otherwise, without written permission from the publisher.

For more information, write to Bearport Publishing, 5357 Penn Avenue South, Minneapolis, MN 55419. Printed in the United States of America.

CONTENTS

The Inside Scoop 4

Locating the Lungs 6

Breathe In............................... 8

Awesome Air 10

Make Way 12

Outstanding Oxygen............. 14

Breathe Out 16

Talk about the Lungs 18

Show Your Lungs Love 20

Your Busy Body..................... 22

Glossary................................. 24

Index 24

THE INSIDE SCOOP

Your body is a super machine that keeps you moving, learning, and having fun. But how does it work? The secret is inside!

Take a big breath, and let's begin!

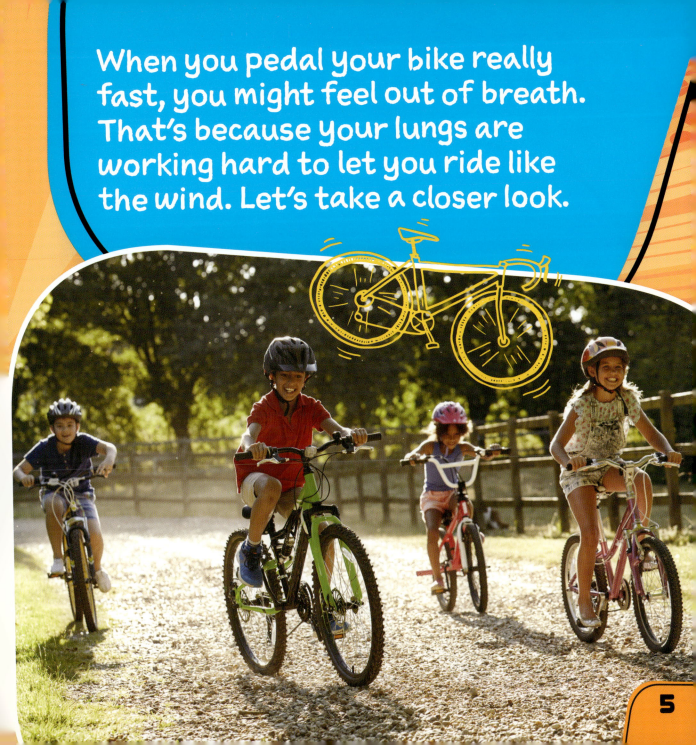

When you pedal your bike really fast, you might feel out of breath. That's because your lungs are working hard to let you ride like the wind. Let's take a closer look.

LOCATING THE LUNGS

You have two lungs to help you breathe. Each one takes up most of the space on either side of your chest.

Your left lung is smaller than your right. It leaves room for your heart!

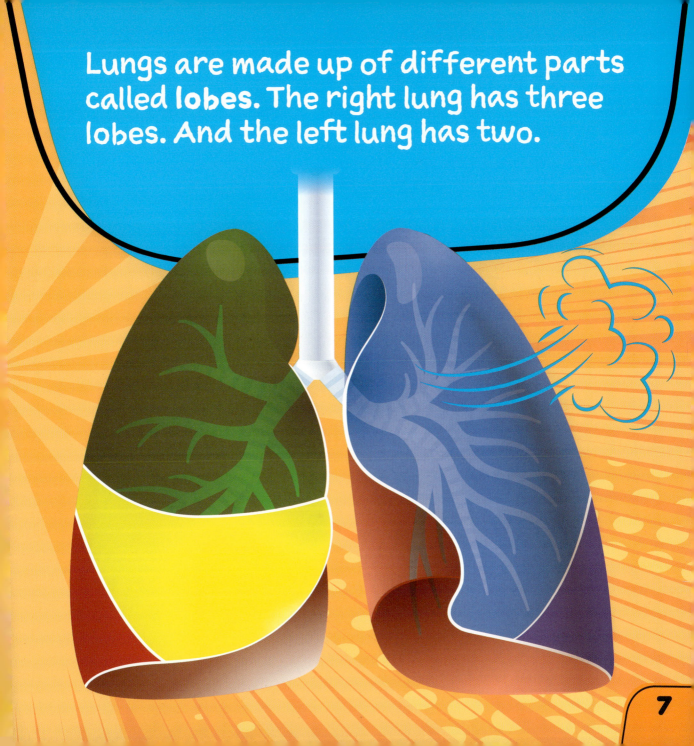
Lungs are made up of different parts called **lobes**. The right lung has three lobes. And the left lung has two.

BREATHE IN

Take a big breath. Air moves in through your nose and mouth. It travels down your throat and through a large tube called the trachea (TRAY-kee-uh).

Tiny hairs in your nose and throat trap dirt from getting to your lungs.

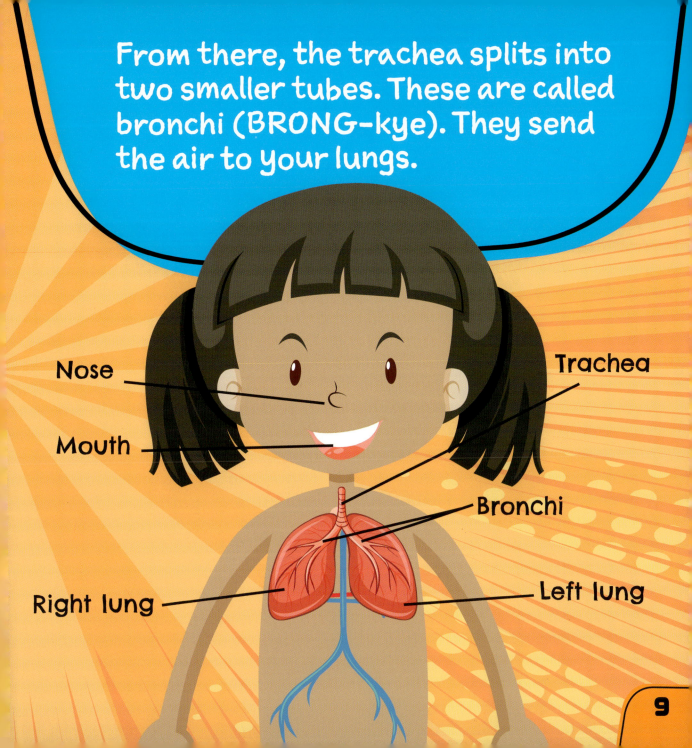

AWESOME AIR

Air enters the lungs and then moves into even tinier tubes. Like the branches of a tree, the tubes get smaller as they go. The smallest are about as thick as a hair.

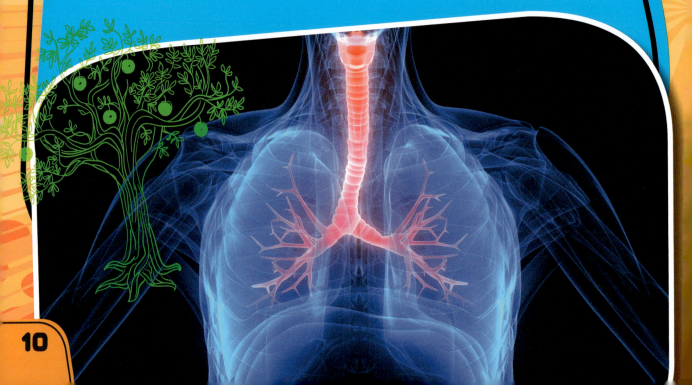

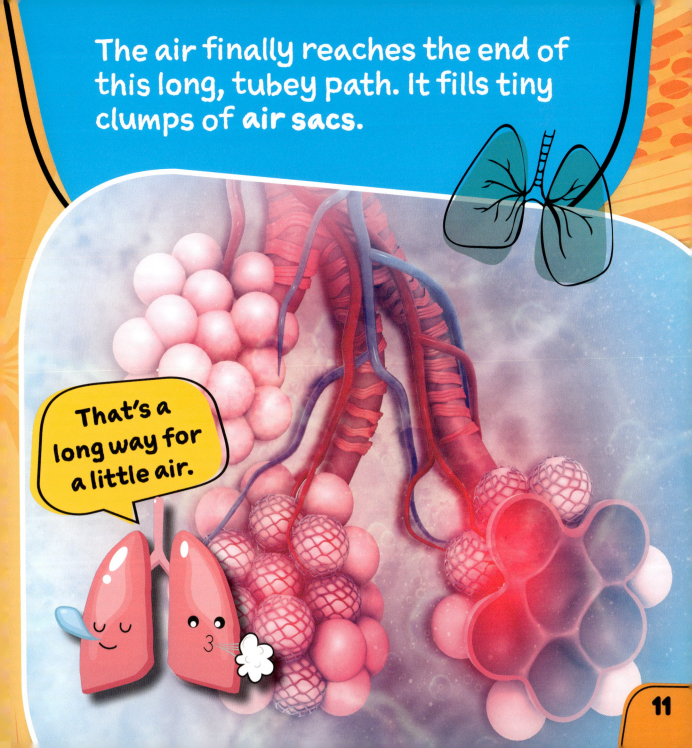

MAKE WAY

Air fills up the space in your lungs. And your body makes room for all that fresh air.

I'm kind of a BIG deal.

12

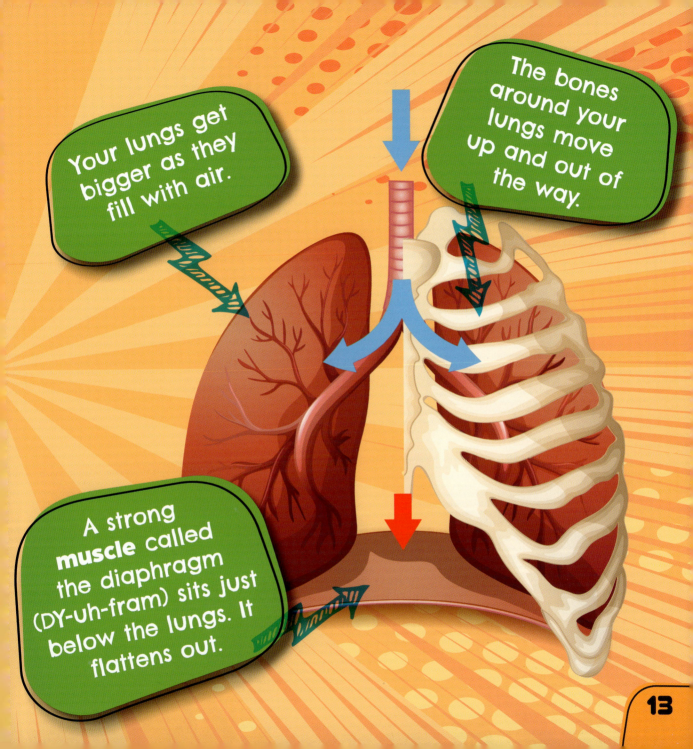

OUTSTANDING OXYGEN

Why do you go through all that work to get air? Because your body needs **oxygen** from the air to do just about everything.

Oxygen travels through your body in your blood.

BREATHE OUT

When your body uses oxygen, it makes some **waste**. How do you get rid of that waste? You breathe out!

It's time to take out the trash!

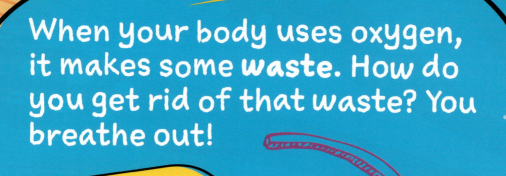

Air comes back out your trachea. It leaves your body through your nose and mouth. And with it, you let out **carbon dioxide**. Then, it's time for your next breath in.

TALK ABOUT THE LUNGS

Your lungs let in oxygen and let out air. But that's not all. They also help you talk.

When you push air out of your lungs, it passes over a voice box in your trachea. Tiny **ridges** on your voice box move to make sound.

The more air you push out, the louder you are.

SHOW YOUR LUNGS LOVE

Your lungs do amazing things for your body. A great way to show your lungs some love is to exercise. It helps make your lungs stronger.

Moving every day will keep your lungs healthy for a long time.

YOUR BUSY BODY

Your lungs are an important part of the super machine that is your body. They work with lots of other things inside you. Together, they keep you going every day!

It's what's on the inside that counts.

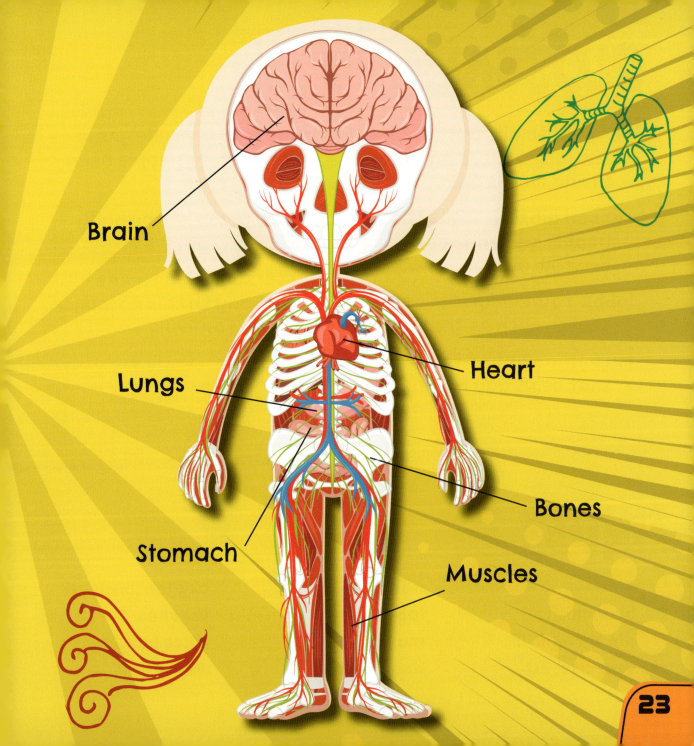

GLOSSARY

air sacs small pouches in the lungs where air comes in and moves out

carbon dioxide a gas that people and animals breathe out

lobes rounded parts of things, such as the lungs

muscle a part of the body that helps you move

oxygen an invisible gas in the air that people need to stay alive

ridges parts of the body with tiny bumps

waste something made by the body that is no longer of use for living

INDEX

air sacs 11

bronchi 9

diaphragm 13

exercise 20

heart 6, 23

lobes 7

mouth 8–9, 17

nose 8–9, 17

oxygen 14–16, 18

trachea 8–9, 17, 19

voice box 19

waste 16